NEVER SAY
May I Help You?

A True-to-Life
Retail Sales Guide

Harold W. Freeman

SALES EFFECTIVENESS TRAINING

Editing, cover and interior design: Peggy Henrikson, Heart and Soul Editing

ISBN-10: 1981951563

ISBN-13: 9781981951567

First Edition
Printed in the United States of America

CONTENTS

INTRODUCTION

The purpose of this guide is to help you become a more effective salesperson. The skills have been presented in the order you would normally use them when working with a customer who's walked into your place of business. This provides you with a more realistic learning experience.

Because it's important for you to know how well you've understood the material that's been presented, self-tests are provided after every unit. The correct answers are given in the back of the book in the Self-Test Answers section.

Important: Write out your answers as this helps you remember what you've read.

Let's begin with Product Knowledge.

UNIT I: PRODUCT KNOWLEDGE

To sell a product successfully, your product knowledge is critical. It refers to your understanding of both the f*eatures* and the ***benefits*** of your products. People buy what a product does for them—its ***benefits.*** They don't buy what it *is*—its ***features.*** A feature is the name or description of something and the ***benefit*** is the advantage or help that the feature provides. Too many salespeople only talk about features, perhaps assuming that the benefits are obvious and that the customer should know what a particular feature does.

> *It's most effective to **sell both the features and benefits of your products.** Don't assume that customers know how a particular feature can be of benefit to them, even if they seem to have familiarity with it.*

One further point: A common mistake many salespeople make is to talk about the product features and benefits ***they*** think are important. If you do this with a customer, you run the risk of losing that person's attention and, worse yet, a sale. So remember, concentrate on selling only those benefits that are important to the ***customer***— the ones that satisfy the customer's needs.

Unit III discusses ways of finding out what a particular customer's needs are.

Before you read on, check your understanding of the material presented so far. On the next page is your first self-test.

SELF-TEST: PRODUCT KNOWLEDGE

1. What do people buy?

    _____

    _____

2. What is a feature?

    _____

    _____

3. What is a benefit?

    _____

    _____

4. What kind of benefits should you talk about?

    _____

    _____

Check your answers with those in the Self-Test Answers section in the back of the book.

PRODUCT PROFILES

On the next page you are going to develop a profile of features and benefits on one of your own products. The product can be any that you choose, but it should be one of the major ones you handle. It could even be your company. List the features and benefits this product offers, why a prospect should do business with you, and so forth.

While doing this profile, keep asking yourself what this product has to offer customers or prospects. What's in it for them or how will it benefit them? Especially list those features and benefits that give you an advantage over your competitors. Keep in mind that you're selling results—what the product will do for someone—not necessarily the product itself.

Now begin developing your product profile. Three profile pages are provided, so you may develop three product profiles if you wish.

Product Profile

Provide the NAME of the product or service you offer:

_____

List the FEATURES of the product or service:

_____

_____

_____

_____

_____

List the BENEFITS of the product or service:

_____

_____

_____

_____

_____

_____

Product Profile

Provide the NAME of the product or service you offer:

_____

List the FEATURES of the product or service:

_____

_____

_____

_____

_____

List the BENEFITS of the product or service:

_____

_____

_____

_____

_____

_____

Product Profile

Provide the NAME of the product or service you offer:

_____

List the FEATURES of the product or service:

_____

_____

_____

_____

_____

List the BENEFITS of the product or service:

_____

_____

_____

_____

_____

_____

UNIT II: APPROACHING PROSPECTS

Approaching and greeting the prospective customer is one of the most important steps in the selling process. It has to be done right.

As you approach some customers, they'll tell you immediately what they're looking for. Many others, however, will hesitate to tell you what they have in mind. Of these, some will not tell you for fear that you will try pressure tactics on them. Others won't tell because they want to look for themselves and decide what they should do before engaging in a conversation.

It's important to realize, however, that unless you can get a customer to talk with you about their wants, needs and/or desires, the odds of selling the customer a product aren't very good. Left on their own, for example, they may look at a product and think the price is too high or it may have too many unnecessary features. They may make any number of faulty assumptions. This could cause them to leave the store before you've had a chance to talk to them. Or it could cause you to try to sell a product that's not suited to their needs, therefore making price the major consideration.

The point is that it's necessary to get your customers or prospects talking in order to increase your chances of selling them.

Following is a formula for approaching customers that increases the chances they'll openly tell you why they happened to walk into your place of business.

> **First:** Identify yourself and ask a question that will get your customer talking.
>
> **Second:** Never say, "May I help you?"

Identifying yourself is a courtesy. It also helps to start a conversation, especially with a new customer. With someone you already know, it's not necessary, of course. In any case, you should do what's most comfortable for you.

The important thing is to ask a question that will get your customer talking. Of course, we're not talking about the old familiar one of "May I help you?" This is the one question you should never use because the customer's response will almost always be, "No, I'm just looking." And that generally ends the conversation.

Certainly the customer is looking for something. But for what? Customers don't walk in the door unless they have something in mind. What is it? It's your job to find out.

How do you do it? By asking a direct question. The kind that makes it hard for a customer to respond with, "No, I'm just looking." Many times you can determine the type of question to ask by observing what the customer is doing.

Next, you'll develop a number of approach statements you might use, depending on the product in question or situation in which you're involved.

First, however, it's time to complete the self-test on the next page.

SELF-TEST: APPROACHING PROSPECTS

1. What is the first rule?

    _____

    _____

2. What is the second rule?

    _____

    _____

    Why?

    _____

    _____

3. Why is it important to get your customers talking?

    _____

    _____

    _____

Check your answers with those in the back of the book.

UNIT III: DETERMINING PROSPECTS' NEEDS

As mentioned, it's important to get your prospective customers to talk with you. This is so you can discover their needs and, in turn, attempt to sell them a product that will satisfy those needs.

Many salespeople, however, make the mistake of assuming that their customers know what they need. As a result, they skip this critical step in the sales process and begin a product presentation. What these people apparently haven't learned yet is that often what customers think they need or say they need is not what they **really** need. Unless the salesperson asks questions to help customers clarify their thinking, i.e., come to the point where they can verbalize what their needs truly are, neither the salesperson nor the customer will be in a position to intelligently discuss the purchase of a product.

When this happens, of course, the customer usually ends up either buying the wrong product or making no purchase at all. In either case, the salesperson loses.

> *Take the time to ask your customers about their needs before you start making a product presentation.* If you do, you'll not only discover their needs, you'll also convince them that you're personally concerned that they make the right buying decision. If you don't, you'll convince them that you're just out to make a sale at any cost.

To be even more specific, make sure you ask and get the answers to the following questions *before* you even think about making a product presentation to customers.

The **key questions** are:

- What is their reason for looking?

- What do they know about your company and its products?

- Have they ever used your products or do they know some-one who has?

- What product are they currently using?

- What's important to them: quality, convenience, performance, price?

By addressing these questions, you may discover, for example, that a customer who came in looking for a low-priced product is really a prospect for a higher-priced one that provides more benefits. So asking appropriate questions will help you sell faster and with less effort. It can also lead to a reduction or elimination of the price objection.

For these reasons and many others, you're encouraged to memorize and use these questions with every customer who walks into your store. Your reward will be increased sales.

Now take the next self-test then check your answers in the back of the book in the Self-Test Answers section.

SELF-TEST: DETERMINING PROSPECTS' NEEDS

Why is it important to ask your prospects about their needs?

a. _____

_____

b. _____

_____

_____

What are the five Key Questions you should always ask?

1. _____

2. _____

3. _____

_____

4. _____

5. _____

_____

UNIT IV: PRESENTING PRODUCTS

Many salespeople seem to think that selling simply involves showing customers several products, hoping they'll pick one out themselves and purchase it. This method works once in a while, of course, but it's not a very effective way of selling. It's time-consuming, and it too often allows the customer to make the wrong buying decision or no buying decision at all.

The most effective salespeople get involved with customers, asking questions to discover their needs. They use the information they gain to recommend the purchase of products they feel will best satisfy those needs.

Once you determine a customer's needs, the next step in the selling process is how to present the product you feel will best satisfy those needs.

Presenting a product is a four-step process:

1. Introduce the product by name.

2. Question for knowledge of the product, if not already known.

3. Show features and benefits that meet customer needs.

4. Ask for acceptance.

The reason it's important to find out whether or not the customer already knows something about the product or has had previous experience with it is so you can determine if the customer has any positive or negative biases toward the product. This allows you to deal with them accordingly—before you begin to discuss the product's features and benefits. Failure to do so decreases your chances of making a sale.

If you fail to discover and deal with a negative bias at this point, you may end up wasting a lot of time and effort trying to convince the customer to buy a product that he or she simply is not going to buy. However, knowing in advance that a customer is favorably disposed toward a product can be a tremendous advantage to you.

To review, the first three steps are:

STEP ONE: *Introduce your product by name.*

STEP TWO: *Probe for knowledge of the product.*

STEP THREE: *Show only those features and benefits of your product that relate directly to the satisfaction of your customer's needs.*

In other words, you don't need or want to describe all of your product's features and benefits to the customer. Just describe those that satisfy the needs the customer has expressed to you. This can benefit you in two ways. First, it saves time. Second, and most important, it eliminates a source of unnecessary objections or concerns.

There is always the possibility, of course, that the customer will express additional needs at this point. If this happens, you'll want to listen carefully to the customer to make sure you fully understand those needs as the person now sees them. This is because you may have to change your strategy. For example, you might have to discuss additional features and benefits of the product you've been presenting. Or you may have to recommend a different product entirely.

In any case, stay alert to what customers are saying and doing. You're there to help them buy the product that's best suited to their needs, and it's not unusual for their ideas on that subject to change from time to time.

STEP FOUR in an effective presentation is to *ask for acceptance.* This gives you an opportunity to find out—before it's too late—whether or not the product you're presenting is acceptable to the customer, in the customer's opinion. You do this by stopping occasionally and asking, "How do you like it so far?" or "Does that suit your needs?" or "What do you think of that?"

If you find out that the product is acceptable, you're well on your way to making a sale. If it's not, you've got a chance to do something about it before it's too late.

One final point about presenting products: Some customers like to be given options when making a major purchase. This gives them the feeling that they are in control of the decision-making process. ***When you feel it's appropriate, by all means give your customers an option*** of buying one or another of your products. This eliminates the possibility that they'll give ***themselves*** the option of buying the product you're presenting or no product at all.

Now you can test what you've just learned about presenting products. Check your answers in the back of the book.

SELF-TEST: PRESENTING PRODUCTS

What are the four steps in a good sales presentation?

1. _____

2. _____

3. _____

   _____

4. _____

When making a product presentation, why is it important to probe for knowledge of that product?

_____

_____

_____

Why is it important NOT to bring up features and benefits that aren't related to your customer's needs?

_____

_____

UNIT V: ASKING FOR THE ORDER

This step in the selling process, *asking for the order,* is given great attention in literature on selling—and perhaps justifiably so because it's a very important step. However, asking for the order is a much simpler step than most "experts" would have you believe. In fact, it's rather **easy.** Here's why. If, through skillful questioning, you have uncovered a customer's needs, **and** you were able to show that customer a product that will meet those needs, **and** the customer agreed that it did, what's more natural than asking for the order—and expecting to get it?

So you see, there's no "trick" to asking for the order or closing the sale. It's something that should follow naturally from an effective sales presentation, which flows naturally from discovery of the customer's needs and meeting those needs. This is another way of saying that there's no such thing as an effective closing in sales; there are only effective salespeople, or people who excel at all steps in the sales process and close lots of sales **as a result.**

> There is only **one rule** when it comes to asking for the order: Do so **when your product presentation has been accepted.**
>
> **How** do you ask for the order? Basically, you can ask in one of two ways:
>
> 1. Directly
> 2. Indirectly, or "forced choice"

Some of you will prefer to ask *directly*. This gives customers an opportunity to decide whether or not they will buy. You might do this by saying:

"Well, how about it? Don't you think this (product name) is the right one for you?"

Others will prefer to ask *indirectly*. This gives customers the *choice* of deciding *which* they will buy, *when* they will buy, or *how* they will buy. *It does not give them a choice as to whether or not they will buy.* To ask for an order indirectly, you might say, "Do you think the standard model will do the job for you, or would you prefer the deluxe one?" Another way is to say, "Do you normally pay cash for something like this or would you prefer our credit program?"

Both methods work; however, one may work better than the other with a certain customer. For example, if you're dealing with a customer who isn't responding either positively or negatively, the indirect or forced choice close—forcing them to decide between two options—is probably the best way to go. At the very least, it guarantees some kind of response and, once you have that, you'll know something of what the customer is feeling or thinking and will thereby be in a better position to know what to do next.

One final thought about asking for orders: *If the customer refuses to buy, don't make the fatal mistake of **suggesting** why the customer didn't buy; rather **ask why** they didn't buy.* For example, a **suggestion** might be: "Do you feel the price is too high?" **Asking** why might be: "Is there something you're concerned about that we haven't discussed?" or "Is there a particular reason you want to wait?"

Now it's time for another self-test. Remember to check the answers.

SELF-TEST: ASKING FOR THE ORDER

When do you ask for the order?

_____

_____

_____

What two types of closes are there?

a. _____

b. _____

Which close is the best?

_____

_____

What kind of close works best with a customer who isn't responding?

_____

_____

_____

_____

UNIT VI: HANDLING RESISTANCE

In retail selling, you will encounter three types of resistance to buying: One is an *objection,* another is *doubt* or *skepticism*, and last, *stalling.*

Objection is opposition or disapproval—some reason to dislike a product that prevents someone from buying it. It's generally something that you can't or won't change. Examples of objections are:

- The price is too high.

- The customer had previous poor experience with a product.

- The product won't do something that's important to the customer.

Doubt or skepticism also prevents customers from buying from you, but it's not something they dislike about the product. Rather, they're uncertain about the product or don't believe that a particular benefit of the product will do what you say it will for them.

Stalling is the third type of resistance. Sometimes customers don't express their objections or doubts. Then when you ask for the order, they stall. Examples of stalling include:

- "I'd like to think it over."

- "I'm going to look around some more."

- "I'm not ready to buy just yet."

- "I'm not sure it really suits my needs."

Following are ways to deal with each type of resistance.

Handling Objections

The steps for handling an objection are:

- Clarify with a question.
- Overcome with benefits.
- Ask for acceptance.

Clarifying the objection is important because often what customers say is not what they mean. Also, we all have a tendency to hear what we want to hear. So before you go on to deal with the objection, be sure you understand exactly what it is.

In clarifying the objection, **rephrase it in the form of a question.** Why a question? A question places you in a neutral position, neither agreeing with an objection nor arguing about it.

For example, if a customer is objecting to what you think is price, you might ask, "Do I understand correctly that you're concerned about the cost of this product?"

Once you've made sure you understand the objection or have clarified it, then you can go on to handle it. Because an objection is something you can't change, you'll have to **overcome it by stressing the benefits of the product.**

Price Objections

The following way to handle price objections has worked quite well for many salespeople.

Initial price is what it costs someone to buy a product. But what's *most important is eventual cost, or what it will cost them to own it.* So initial price should only be a minor consideration and eventual cost the major consideration.

Eventual Cost

Even though a product may cost less to begin with than others, the customer needs to consider such factors as:

- Frequency of replacement
- Cost of parts
- Cost of maintenance
- Design features

The type of material used will have a bearing on cost of ownership. Of course, many more factors need to be considered. Prepare a list of them so you'll be able to discuss them with your customers when the situation calls for it.

Furthermore, averaging the difference in price between two similar products over the useful life of those products often results in a tiny difference per year. For example, if the product in question has a useful life of ten years, divide the selling price by ten and compare it to the same calculation for a lesser priced product. This will make the difference look considerably smaller.

The **final step** in handling an objection is to ***ask for acceptance.*** Were you able to overcome the objection with the benefits? Ask a question such as: "So can you see that the additional cost is well justified?"

Handling Doubt or Skepticism

The steps in handling doubt or skepticism are:

- Clarify with a question.
- Provide proof.
- Ask for acceptance.

As in handling objections, ***clarifying the doubt*** is important because you want to be sure you understand exactly what your customer doubts or is skeptical about before you try to offer proof. Remember, you're dealing with a benefit that's important to your customer; otherwise he or she wouldn't be questioning it. It could also be critical to getting the sale, so don't assume you know what your customer is saying. Ask. Clarify.

Again, you clarify by rephrasing the objection in the form of a question. For example, "If I understand you correctly, you don't think our equipment will hold up well, right?" Or, "If I hear you correctly, you doubt that we'll provide the service we say we will. Is that it?"

By rephrasing in question form, you are also qualifying the prospect. If the benefit under discussion is of great importance to your prospect and you can prove it will be provided, you will likely be able to conclude the sale.

The next step after clarifying is to **offer proof that your product will provide the benefit** you say it will. You can do this in a variety of ways, such as the following:

- **Demonstrate** the product to provide visible and **tangible proof** of a product's benefits.

- Use **third-party references** from good customers of yours who are pleased with the products or services you offer.

- Provide **product literature, specification sheets, videos, pictures, or any other tangible thing** that will help back up your claims.

The last step in handling doubt or skepticism is to **ask for acceptance of your proof.** Ask a question such as, "Does that take care of your concern?" or "Does that answer your question?"

Handling Stalling

To handle a stalling prospect, you need to **ask about the reason for the stalling.** For example, ask questions such as: "Could you tell me why you're not ready to buy yet?" "Is there some particular reason you're hesitating to buy?" or "Is there something you're concerned about?"

As mentioned earlier, stalling customers are those who put you off or refuse to buy when you ask for the order. They generally have an objection or doubt that hasn't been expressed. In some cases, their stalling may be legitimate. They may want to look around to make sure they're making the right decision.

Once you (and the customer) are clear about the reason for the stalling, you can address it.

Now go on to the next page and complete the final self-test.

SELF-TEST: HANDLING RESISTANCE

What is an objection?

_____

_____

_____

How do you handle an objection?

a. _____

b. _____

c. _____

What is a doubt or skepticism?

_____

_____

_____

How do you handle a doubt or skepticism?

a. _____

b. _____

c. _____

Why do people stall?

_____

_____

How do you handle a stall?

_____

_____

FINAL EXERCISE

For the final exercise, list the objections you hear the most in the left column and ways to handle them in the right column. Use as many lines in the right column as you need for each objection in the left column.

OBJECTIONS	WAYS TO HANDLE

OBJECTIONS	WAYS TO HANDLE

SELF-TEST ANSWERS

SELF-TEST ANSWERS: PRODUCT KNOWLEDGE

What do people buy?

The benefits of a product

What is a feature?

The name or description of something

What is a benefit?

The advantage or help that a particular feature provides

What kind of benefits should you talk about?

Only those that are of interest to the customer and that meet the customer's expressed needs

SELF-TEST ANSWERS: APPROACHING PROSPECTS

What is the first rule?

Identify yourself and ask a question that gets your customer or prospect talking.

What is the second rule?

Never say, "May I help you?" to customers because they generally will say, "No, I'm just looking," and the conversation will end.

Why is it important to get your customers talking?

So you can determine their needs, wants and/or desires which, in turn, makes it easier for you to sell to them

SELF-TEST ANSWERS: DETERMINING PROSPECTS' NEEDS

Why is it important for you to ask your customers about their needs?

> a. *To help them clarify their thinking*
>
> b. *To understand their true needs so you can recommend the right product, which increases your chance of making the sale*
>
> c. *To make your selling job easier*

What five key questions should you always ask?

> 1. *Why are they looking?*
>
> 2. *What do they know about your company and its products?*
>
> 3. *Have they ever used your products or do they know someone who has?*
>
> 4. *What product are they currently using?*
>
> 5. *What's important to them: quality, convenience, performance, price?*

SELF-TEST ANSWERS: PRESENTING PRODUCTS

What are the four steps in a good sales presentation?

1. *Introduce the product by name.*

2. *Question for knowledge of the product if not already known.*

3. *Show features and benefits that meet customer needs.*

4. *Ask for acceptance.*

When making a product presentation, why is it important to probe for knowledge of that product?

To see if the customer has had any prior experience, good or bad, with the product or something similar.

Why is it important NOT to bring up features and benefits that aren't related to your customer's needs?

It could open up objections or concerns about their value.

SELF-TEST ANSWERS: ASKING FOR THE ORDER

When do you ask for the order?

When your presentation has been accepted

What two types of closes are there?

1. *Direct*
2. *Indirect or "forced choice"*

Which close is the best?

It depends on your style or the situation.

What kind of close works best with a customer who isn't responding?

The forced choice

SELF-TEST ANSWERS: HANDLING RESISTANCE

What is an objection?

Opposition, disapproval, or some reason to dislike a product that prevents someone from buying it, which is generally something you can't or won't change.

How do you handle an objection?

> *a. Clarify with a question.*
>
> *b. Overcome with benefits.*
>
> *c. Ask for acceptance.*

What is a doubt or skepticism?

Uncertainty about a particular benefit

How do you handle a doubt or skepticism?

> *a. Clarify the doubt.*
>
> *b. Offer proof.*
>
> *c. Ask for acceptance.*

Why do people stall?

They generally have a hidden objection or doubt.

How do you handle a stall?

Question for the reason so you know how to address it.

Congratulations! You now know a simple, true-to-life approach to effective retail selling. Watch your sales soar!

ABOUT THE AUTHOR

Harold W. Freeman has more than 60 years in sales under his belt. Few can claim the depth and breadth of his sales and sales training experience. He has sold door to door as well as on a retail sales floor. While in sales and sales management with 3M, IBM, Honeywell, and Xerox, he sold to a host of businesses and industries.

For six years, Harold served as vice president of a Xerox Learning Center and custom sales training firm and served clients such as John Deere, Marion Laboratories, Watkins Company, and The Toro Company.

Eventually, he formed his own company, S.E.T. Incorporated, to offer additional services to his clients that capitalized on his many years of sales, management, and training experience. He wrote *The Sales Process* training program used by a multitude of major U.S. corporations, such as Cargill, Sun Financial Group, Fuji Photo Film, and American Express. Among others, his client list also included 3M, NASA, ITT Consumer Financial Corporation, and the U.S. Navy Organizational Effectiveness Command.

Harold has been an active member of and leader in Sales and Marketing Executives, and for six years, he served on the board of directors of the Professional Sales Association. He has advised and lectured at the University of Minnesota, community colleges, and many professional organizations. Directly or indirectly, he's been responsible for the sales training of over 10,000 salespeople in every type of sales environment.

Harold's philosophy is that an effective sales training program must be easy to learn, simple to remember, and true to life.

www.ingramcontent.com/pod-product-compliance
Lightning Source LLC
Chambersburg PA
CBHW081645220526
45468CB00009B/2562